Everything You Need to Know to Prevent, Identify, and Respond to Identity Theft

Everything You Need to Know to Prevent, Identify, and Respond to Identity Theft

Diane M. Pfadenhauer

Everything You Need to Know to Prevent, Identify, and Respond to Identity Theft

Copyright © 2012 Diane M. Pfadenhauer

All rights reserved. No part of this book may be reproduced in any form without permission from the author, except by a reviewer. The reviewer may quote brief passages to be printed in a newspaper or magazine.

Table of Contents

WARNING–DISCLAIMER 5

INTRODUCTION 7

CHAPTER 1 - THE PROBLEM 9
   FEDERAL AND STATE LAW 11

CHAPTER 2 - NOTICING YOUR IDENTITY HAS
BEEN STOLEN AND HOW IT OCCURS 13
   HOW THIEVES GET YOUR INFORMATION 14
   HOW THIEVES USE YOUR INFORMATION 15

CHAPTER 3 - IMMEDIATE ACTION STEPS 17
   IMMEDIATE ACTION STEPS IF YOUR INFORMATION IS
   STOLEN OR LOST 17
      Financial Accounts 17
      Social Security number 18
      Driver's license/other government-issued
      identification 18
   SPECIFIC STEPS TO TAKE IF YOU BELIEVE YOUR
   IDENTITY HAS BEEN STOLEN 18
      Place Fraud Alerts on Your Credit Reports 18
      Review Your Credit Reports 20
      Close Accounts that You Believe have been
      Compromised or Opened Fraudulently 20

Everything You Need to Know About Identity Theft

  How to Prove You are a Victim 22
  File a Police Report 23
  File a Complaint with the Federal Trade Commission
  23
 WHAT IS AN IDENTITY THEFT REPORT? 24
  Part One 24
  Part Two 24
 IMPORTANT GUIDELINES FOR ORGANIZING YOUR CASE 25

CHAPTER 4 - SPECIFIC PROBLEMS 27

 FRAUDULENT WITHDRAWALS FROM BANK ACCOUNTS ... 27
 FRAUDULENT ELECTRONIC WITHDRAWALS 28
 FRAUDULENT CHECKS 29
 FRAUDULENT NEW ACCOUNTS 31
 BANKRUPTCY FRAUD 32
 WHEN FINANCIAL INSTITUTIONS ARE UNCOOPERATIVE 33
 CORRECTING CREDIT REPORTS 34
 CREDIT CARD PROBLEMS 36
 CRIMINAL VIOLATIONS 38
 DEBT COLLECTORS 40
 YOUR DRIVER'S LICENSE 41
 INVESTMENT FRAUD 42
 MAIL FRAUD 42
 PASSPORT FRAUD 43
 TELEPHONE FRAUD 43
 SOCIAL SECURITY NUMBER FRAUD AND MISUSE 44
 STUDENT LOANS 44
 TAX FRAUD 44
 MEDICAL IDENTITY THEFT 45
  Preventing Medical Identity Theft 46
  Detecting Medical Identity Theft 47

CHAPTER 5 - ONGOING VIGILANCE 51

 GET YOUR CREDIT REPORTS 52
 ADDITIONAL REPORTS 53

ii

Everything You Need to Know About Identity Theft

ACTIVE ALERTS FOR MILITARY PERSONNEL.................. 53
PREVENTION IS KEY 54
   Guard Your Personal Information 54
   Guard Your Mail and Trash 56
   Your Personal Belongings... 56
   Sharing Your Social Security Number...................... 57
   Protecting Your Credit, ATM and Debit Cards 58
   Computers and the Internet 60
   Using Public Wireless Networks 62
   Products and Services for Purchase......................... 65
   Fraud Alerts... 65
   Credit Freezes.. 67
   Identity Theft Protection Products and Services for Sale... 68

CHAPTER 6 - COMPLETING AN IDENTITY THEFT AFFIDAVIT.. 71
   Instructions 72

SAMPLE LETTERS.. 75
   Sample Blocking Letter to Consumer Reporting Agency... 75
   Sample Dispute Letter for Fraudulent Charge on Credit or Debit Card.. 76

IDENTITY THEFT AFFIDAVIT 77

iii

Warning–Disclaimer

While this book strives to provide the reader with practical guidance and to provide general education on the topic at hand, it is not a substitute for adequate legal or other professional advice. The opinions within represent the opinions of the authors and editors only and, therefore, should not be construed as a position on the part of any particular organization or entity.

Further, nothing herein should be construed as the rendering of legal or other professional advice and the reader is advised to consult with appropriate counsel for obtaining any advice. By reading this publication, no attorney client relationship exists between the reader and either the author or publisher.

Introduction

In the course of a busy day, you may write a check at the grocery store, charge tickets to a ball game, rent a car, mail your tax returns, change service providers for your cell phone, or apply for a credit card. Chances are you don't give these everyday transactions a second thought. But an identity thief does.

As the public moves online to execute financial transactions, make purchases, and create online accounts, the problem has the potential to magnify. Identity theft is a serious crime. People whose identities have been stolen can spend months or years — and thousands of dollars — cleaning up the mess the thieves have made of a good name and credit record. In the meantime, victims of identity theft may lose job opportunities, find their credit compromised, be refused loans for education, housing, or cars, be refused employment and even get arrested for crimes they didn't commit. Humiliation, anger, and frustration are among the feelings victims experience as they navigate the process of rescuing their identity.

This book describes what steps to take, your legal rights, how to handle specific problems you may encounter on the way to clearing your name, and what to watch for in the future.

1

The Problem

Identity theft involves the misuse of another individual's personal identifying information for fraudulent purposes. It is almost always committed to facilitate other crimes, such as credit card fraud, mortgage fraud, and check fraud. Personal identifying information, such as name, Social Security number (SSN), date of birth and bank account number is extremely valuable to an identity thief. With relatively little effort, an identity thief can use this information to take over existing credit accounts, create new accounts in the victim's name or even evade law enforcement after the commission of a violent crime. Identity thieves also sell personal information online to the highest bidder, often resulting in the stolen information being used by a number of different perpetrators. Identity theft can be very difficult for consumers to deal with, as they often do not know they have been defrauded until they are denied credit or receive a call from a creditor seeking payment for a debt incurred in their name.

Although not a new crime, identity theft has evolved into a serious and pervasive threat to consumers and the financial services industry alike. Estimates vary on the true impact of the problem, but law enforcement and consumer advocacy groups agree that financial institutions lose billions of dollars each year to identity theft and consumers face additional hardships, ranging from financial loss to time spent trying to undo the harm caused to their credit records and other aspects of their lives. Identity theft also puts significant demands on law enforcement, as federal, state, and local law enforcement agencies and prosecutors grapple with venue issues and limited resources, which can complicate their efforts to effectively deal with the problem.

A survey conducted by the Federal Trade Commission (FTC) in 2006 estimated that 8.3 million American consumers, or 3.7 percent of the adult population, became victims of identity theft in 2005. Most of the financial losses are suffered by credit issuers and banks, as victims are rarely held responsible for fraudulent debts incurred in their name; however, victims often bear the responsibility of contacting their banks and credit issuers after an identity theft has occurred. The same FTC survey determined that victim consumers spent over 200 million hours in 2005 attempting to recover from identity theft.

> *Fact:*
> *8.3 million American consumers, or 3.7 percent of the adult population, became victims of identity theft in 2005.*

Law enforcement agencies across the country have formed task forces and working groups to address the identity theft problem. The FBI currently participates in 21 task forces and working groups dedicated to identity theft and over 80 other financial crimes task forces. In cities such as Detroit, Chicago, Los Angeles, and Salt Lake City, identity fraud task forces are realizing significant success. For example, in FY 2005 the Detroit Metropolitan Identity Fraud Task Force accumulated the following statistical accomplishments: 23 search warrants, 23 arrest warrants, 37 arrests, 11 indictments, 29 convictions, 69 fraud cells identified, and 23 identity fraud organizations dismantled. In addition, the FBI has dedicated significant analytical resources to combating the identity theft problem and is working with the President's Identity Theft Task Force and other agencies such as the FTC to develop a system that will analyze large streams of identity theft data and refer the results to law enforcement agencies in order to proactively target organized groups of identity thieves.

> *Fact:*
> *Many states have passed laws making identity theft a crime or providing help in recovery from identity theft; others are considering such legislation.*

Although the total number of FBI identity theft-related cases has decreased from 1,678 in FY 2005 to 1,255 in FY 2006, its field offices have been aggressively pursuing identity theft charges in many of our investigations, ranging from traditional bank fraud cases to counterterrorism cases.

Federal and State Law

The Identity Theft and Assumption Deterrence Act, enacted by Congress in October 1998 (and codified, in part, at 18 U.S.C. §1028) makes identity theft a federal crime.

Under federal criminal law, identity theft takes place when someone "knowingly transfers, possesses or uses, without lawful authority, a means of identification of another person with the intent to commit, or to aid or abet, or in connection with, any unlawful activity that constitutes a violation of federal law, or that constitutes a felony under any applicable state or local law."

Under this definition, a name or Social Security number is considered a "means of identification." So is a credit card number, cellular telephone electronic serial number, or any other piece of information that may be used alone or in conjunction with other information to identify a specific individual.

Violations of the federal crime are investigated by federal law enforcement agencies, including the U.S. Secret Service, the FBI, the U.S. Postal Inspection Service, and the Social Security Administration's Office of the Inspector General. Federal identity theft cases are prosecuted by the U.S. Department of Justice.

For the purposes of the law, the FCRA defines identity theft to apply to consumers and businesses.

Many states have passed laws making identity theft a crime or providing help in recovery from identity theft; others are considering such legislation. Where specific criminal identity theft laws do not exist, the practices may be prohibited under other laws. Contact your state Attorney General (for a list of state offices, visit www.naag.org) or local consumer protection agency for laws related to identity theft.

2

Noticing Your Identity has been Stolen and how it Occurs

The following occurrences are some of the indications of identity theft:

- Charges occurring on your accounts that you did not authorize.
- If your credit is denied due to poor credit ratings, despite good credit history.
- If you are contacted by creditors regarding amounts owed for goods or services that you never obtained or authorized.
- If your credit card and bank statements are not received in the mail as expected.
- If a new or renewed credit card is not received.

How Thieves Get Your Information

Identity thieves can obtain your information in a variety of ways. These include:

1. Getting information from businesses or other institutions by:
    - stealing records or information while they're on the job
    - bribing an employee who has access to these records
    - hacking these records
    - conning information out of employees

2. Stealing your mail, including bank and credit card statements, credit card offers, new checks, and tax information.

3. Rummaging through your trash, the trash of businesses, or public trash dumps in a practice known as "dumpster diving."

4. Obtaining your credit reports by abusing their employer's authorized access to them, or by posing as a landlord, employer, or someone else who may have a legal right to access your report.

5. Stealing your credit or debit card numbers by capturing the information in a data storage device in a practice known as "skimming." They may swipe your card for an actual purchase, or attach the device to an ATM machine where you may enter or swipe your card.

6. Stealing your wallet or purse.

7. Stealing personal information they find in your home.

8. Stealing personal information from you through email or phone by posing as legitimate companies and claiming that you have a problem with your account. This practice is known as "phishing" online, or "pretexting" by phone.

How Thieves Use Your Information

Identity thieves will use your information in a variety of ways:

1. They may call your credit card issuer to change the billing address on your credit card account. The imposter then runs up charges on your account. Because your bills are being sent to a different address, it may be some time before you realize there's a problem.

2. They may open new credit card accounts in your name. When they use the credit cards and don't pay the bills, the delinquent accounts are reported on your credit report.

3. They may establish phone or wireless service in your name.

4. They may open a bank account in your name and write bad checks on that account.

5. They may counterfeit checks or credit or debit cards, or authorize electronic transfers in your name, and drain your bank account.

6. They may file for bankruptcy under your name to avoid paying debts they've incurred under your name, or to avoid eviction.

7. They may buy a car by taking out an auto loan in your name.

8. They may get identification such as a driver's license issued with their picture, in your name.

9. They may get a job or file fraudulent tax returns in your name.

10. They may give your name to the police during an arrest. If they don't show up for their court date, a warrant for arrest is issued in your name.

3

Immediate Action Steps

Immediate Action Steps if Your Information Is Stolen or Lost

If you've lost personal information or identification, or if it has been stolen from you, taking certain steps quickly can minimize the potential for identity theft.

Financial Accounts

Close accounts, like credit cards and bank accounts, immediately. When you open new accounts, place passwords on them. Avoid using your mother's maiden name, your birth date, the last four digits of your Social Security number (SSN) or your phone number, or a series of consecutive numbers.

Social Security number

Call the toll-free fraud number of any of the three nationwide consumer reporting companies and place an initial fraud alert on your credit reports. An alert can help stop someone from opening new credit accounts in your name.

Driver's license/other government-issued identification

Contact the agency that issued the license or other identification document. Follow its procedures to cancel the document and to get a replacement. Ask the agency to flag your file so that no one else can get a license or any other identification document from them in your name.

Once you've taken these precautions, watch for signs that your information is being misused.

If your information has been misused, file a report about the theft with the police, and file a complaint with the Federal Trade Commission, as well. If another crime was committed – for example, if your purse or wallet was stolen or your house or car was broken into – report it to the police immediately.

Specific Steps to Take if You Believe Your Identity Has Been Stolen

Place Fraud Alerts on Your Credit Reports

Fraud alerts can help prevent an identity thief from opening any more accounts in your name. Contact the toll-free fraud number of any of the three consumer reporting companies to place a fraud alert on your credit report. You only need to contact one of the three companies to place an alert. The company you call is required to contact the other two, which will place an alert on their versions of your report, too.

There are two types of fraud alerts:

Initial Alert - An initial alert stays on your credit report for at least 90 days. You may ask that an initial fraud alert be placed on your credit report if you suspect you have been, or are about to be, a victim of identity theft. An initial alert is appropriate if your wallet has been stolen or if you've been taken in by a "phishing" scam. When you place an initial fraud alert on your credit report, you're entitled to one free credit report from each of the three nationwide consumer reporting companies.

Extended Alert - An extended alert stays on your credit report for seven years. You can have an extended alert placed on your credit report if you've been a victim of identity theft and you provide the consumer reporting company with an "identity theft report". When you place an extended alert on your credit report, you're entitled to two free credit reports within 12 months from each of the three nationwide consumer reporting companies. In addition, the consumer reporting companies will remove your name from marketing lists for pre-screened credit offers for five years – unless you ask them to put your name back on the list before then.

To place either of these alerts on your credit report, you will be required to provide appropriate proof of your identity, which may include your SSN, name, address and other personal information requested by the consumer reporting company. To remove the fraud alert, you will need a copy of an identity theft report and proof of your identity.

Everything You Need to Know About Identity Theft

When a business sees the alert on your credit report, they must verify your identity before issuing you credit. As part of this verification process, the business may try to contact you directly. This may cause some delays if you're trying to obtain credit.

To compensate for possible delays, you may wish to include a cell phone number, where you can be reached easily, in your alert. Remember to keep all contact information in your alert current.

Once you place the fraud alert in your file, you're entitled to order free copies of your credit reports, and, if you ask, only the last four digits of your SSN will appear on your credit reports.

Review Your Credit Reports

Once you receive your credit reports, review them carefully. Look for inquiries from companies you haven't contacted, accounts you didn't open, and debts on your accounts that you can't explain. Check that information like your SSN, address(es), name or initials, and employers are correct. If you find fraudulent or inaccurate information, get it removed. Continue to check your credit reports periodically, especially for the first year after you discover the identity theft, to make sure no new fraudulent activity has occurred.

> *Fact:*
> *Once you place the fraud alert in your Credit file, you're entitled to order free copies of your credit reports.*

Close Accounts that You Believe have been Compromised or Opened Fraudulently

Call and speak with someone in the security or fraud department of each company. Follow up *in writing*, and include copies (NOT originals) of supporting documents. It's important to notify credit card companies and banks in writing. Send your letters by certified mail, return receipt requested, so you can document what the company received and when. Keep a file of your correspondence and enclosures.

When you open new accounts, use new Personal Identification Numbers (PINs) and passwords. Avoid using easily available information like your mother's maiden name, your birth date, the last four digits of your SSN or your phone number, or a series of consecutive numbers.

If the identity thief has made charges or debits on your accounts, or on fraudulently opened accounts, ask the company for the forms to dispute those transactions.

For charges and debits on existing accounts, ask the representative to send you the company's fraud dispute forms. If the company doesn't have special forms, use the sample letter provided later in this guide to dispute the fraudulent charges or debits. In either case, write to the company at the address given for "billing inquiries," NOT the address for sending your payments.

For new unauthorized accounts, ask if the company accepts the ID Theft Affidavit. If not, ask the representative to send you the company's fraud dispute forms.

If the company already has reported these accounts or debts on your credit report, dispute this fraudulent information. See the session in this book regarding correcting credit reports to learn how.

Once you have resolved your identity theft dispute with the company, ask for a letter stating that the company has closed the disputed accounts and has discharged the fraudulent debts. This letter is your best proof if errors relating to this account reappear on your credit report or you are contacted again about the fraudulent debt.

How to Prove You are a Victim

Applications or other transaction records related to the theft of your identity may help you prove that you are a victim. For example, you may be able to show that the signature on an application is not yours. These documents also may contain information about the identity thief that is valuable to law enforcement. By law, companies *must* give you a copy of the application or other business transaction records relating to your identity theft if you submit your request in writing. Be sure to ask the company representative where you should mail your request. Companies must provide these records at no charge to you within 30 days of receipt of your request and your supporting documents. You also may give permission to any law enforcement agency to get these records, or ask in your written request that a copy of these records be sent to a particular law enforcement officer.

> *Fact:*
> *Companies must give you a copy of the application or other business transaction records relating to your identity theft if you submit your request in writing*

The company can ask you for proof of your identity. This may be a photocopy of a government-issued identification card, the same type of information the identity thief used to open or access the account, or the type of information the company usually requests from applicants or customers.

The company can also ask you for a police report and a completed affidavit, which may be the Identity Theft Affidavit or the company's own affidavit.

File a Police Report

File a report with your local police or the police in the community where the identity theft took place. Thus, for example, if you were on vacation and your wallet was stolen, you would want to file a police report where you were on vacation. Then, get a copy of the police report or at the very least, the number of the report. It can help you deal with creditors who need proof of the crime. If the police are reluctant to take your report, ask to file a "Miscellaneous Incidents" report, or try another jurisdiction, like your state police. You also can check with your state Attorney General's office to find out if state law requires the police to take reports for identity theft. You can often find this information in the Blue Pages of your local telephone directory for the phone number or check www.naag.org for a list of state Attorneys General.

File a Complaint with the Federal Trade Commission

By sharing your identity theft complaint with the FTC, you will provide important information that can help law enforcement officials across the nation track down identity thieves and stop them. The FTC can refer victims' complaints to other government agencies and companies for further action, as well as investigate companies for violations of laws the agency enforces.

> *Tip:*
> *By sharing your identity theft complaint with the FTC, you will provide important information that can help law enforcement officials across the nation track down identity thieves and stop them.*

You can file a complaint online at www.ftc.gov/idtheft. If you don't have Internet access, call the FTC's Identity Theft Hotline, toll-free: 1-877-

IDTHEFT (1-877-438-4338); TTY: 1-866-653-4261; or write: Identity Theft Clearinghouse, Federal Trade Commission, 600 Pennsylvania Avenue, NW, Washington, DC 20580.

Be sure to call the Hotline to update your complaint if you have any additional information or problems.

What is an Identity Theft Report?

Generally, an identity theft report has two parts.

Part One

Part one is a copy of a report filed with a local, state, or federal law enforcement agency, like the local police department, your State Attorney General, the FBI, the U.S. Secret Service, the FTC, and the U.S. Postal Inspection Service. There is no federal law requiring a federal agency to take a report about identity theft; however, some state laws require local police departments to take reports. When you file a report, provide as much information as you can about the crime, including anything you know about the dates of the identity theft, the fraudulent accounts opened, and the alleged identity thief.

Part Two

Part two of an identity theft report depends on the policies of the consumer reporting company and the information provider (the business that sent the information to the consumer reporting company). That is, they may ask you to provide information or documentation in addition to that included in the law enforcement report which is reasonably intended to verify your identity theft. They must make their request within 15 days of receiving your law enforcement report, or, if you already obtained an extended fraud alert on your credit report, the date you submit your request to the credit reporting company for information blocking. The consumer reporting company and information provider then have 15 more days to work with you to make sure your identity theft report contains everything they need. They are entitled to take five days to review any information you give them. For example, if you give them information 11 days after they request it, they do not have to make a final decision until 16 days after they asked you for that information. If you give them any information after the 15-day deadline, they can reject your identity theft report as incomplete; you will have to resubmit your identity theft report with the correct information.

Most federal and state agencies, and some local police departments, offer only "automated" reports – a report that does not require a face-to-face meeting with a law enforcement officer. Automated reports may be submitted online, or by telephone or mail. If you have a choice, do not use an automated report. Why? It is more difficult for the consumer reporting company or information provider to verify the information. Unless you are asking a consumer reporting company to place an extended fraud alert on your credit report, you probably will have to provide additional information or documentation when you use an automated report

Important Guidelines for Organizing Your Case

Accurate and complete records will help you to resolve your identity theft case more quickly.

Have a plan when you contact a company. Don't assume that the person you talk to will give you all the information or help you need. Prepare a list of questions to ask the representative, as well as information about your identity theft. Don't end the call until you're sure you understand everything you've been told. If you need more help, ask to speak to a supervisor.

Write down the name of everyone you talk to, what he or she tells you, and the date the conversation occurred. Keep a comprehensive log of your activities.

Follow up in writing with all contacts you've made on the phone or in person. Use certified mail, return receipt requested, so you can document what the company or organization received and when.

> *Tip:*
> *Keep the originals of supporting documents, like police reports and letters to and from creditors; send copies only.*

Keep copies of all correspondence or forms you send.

Keep the originals of supporting documents, like police reports and letters to and from creditors; send copies only.

Set up a filing system for easy access to your paperwork.

Keep old files even if you believe your case is closed. Once resolved, most cases stay resolved, but problems can crop up.

4

Specific Problems

While dealing with problems resulting from identity theft can be time-consuming and frustrating, most victims can resolve their cases by being assertive, organized, and knowledgeable about their legal rights. Some laws require you to notify companies within specific time periods. Don't delay in contacting any companies to deal with these problems, and ask for supervisors if you need more help than you're getting.

Fraudulent Withdrawals from Bank Accounts

It is important to note that different laws determine your legal remedies based on the type of bank fraud you have suffered. For example, state laws protect you against fraud committed by a thief using paper documents, like stolen or counterfeit checks. But if the thief used an electronic fund transfer, federal law applies. Many transactions may seem to be processed electronically but are still considered "paper" transactions. If you're not sure what type of transaction the thief used to commit the fraud, ask the financial institution that processed the transaction.

Fraudulent Electronic Withdrawals

The Electronic Fund Transfer Act provides consumer protections for transactions involving an ATM or debit card, or another electronic way to debit or credit an account. It also limits your liability for unauthorized electronic fund transfers.

Fact: The Electronic Fund Transfer Act provides consumer protections for transactions involving an ATM or debit card, or another electronic way to debit or credit an account.

You have 60 days from the date your bank account statement is sent to you to report in writing any money withdrawn from your account without your permission. This includes instances when your ATM or debit card is "skimmed" – that is, when a thief captures your account number and PIN without your card having been lost or stolen.

If your ATM or debit card is lost or stolen, report it immediately because the amount you can be held responsible for depends on how quickly you report the loss.

- If you report the loss or theft within two business days of discovery, your losses are limited to $50.
- If you report the loss or theft after two business days, but within 60 days after the unauthorized electronic fund transfer appears on your statement, you could lose up to $500 of what the thief withdraws.
- If you wait more than 60 days to report the loss or theft, you could lose all the money that was taken from your account after the end of the 60 days.

- Most card issuers voluntarily have agreed to limit or waive consumers' liability for unauthorized use of their debit cards, no matter how much time has elapsed since the discovery of the loss or theft of the card. Contact your card issuer for more information.

The best way to protect yourself in the event of an error or fraudulent transaction is to call the financial institution and follow up in writing – by certified letter, return receipt requested – so you can prove when the institution received your letter. Keep a copy of the letter you send for your records.

After receiving your notification about an error on your statement, the institution generally has 10 business days to investigate. The institution must tell you the results of its investigation within three business days after completing it and must correct an error within one business day after determining that it occurred. If the institution needs more time, it may take up to 45 days to complete the investigation – but only if the money in dispute is returned to your account and you are notified promptly of the credit. At the end of the investigation, if no error has been found, the institution may take the money back if it sends you a written explanation.

Fraudulent Checks

If an identity thief steals your checks or counterfeits checks from your existing bank account, stop payment, close the account, and ask your bank to notify Chex Systems, Inc. or the check verification service with which it does business. That way, retailers can be notified not to accept these checks. While no federal law limits your losses if someone uses your checks with a forged signature, or uses another type of "paper" transaction such as a demand draft, state laws may protect you. Most states hold the bank responsible for losses from such transactions. At the same time, most states require you to take reasonable care of your account. For example, you may be held responsible for the forgery if you fail to notify the bank in a timely manner that a check was lost or stolen. Contact your state banking or consumer protection agency for more information.

The following are the major check verification companies which you can contact directly for the following services:

- To request that they notify retailers who use their databases not to accept your checks, call TeleCheck at 1-800-710-9898 or 1-800-927-0188 or Certegy, Inc. (previously Equifax Check Systems) at 1-800-437-5120.
- To find out if the identity thief has been passing bad checks in your name, call SCAN at 1-800-262-7771.

If your checks are rejected by a merchant, it may be because an identity thief is using the Magnetic Information Character Recognition (MICR) code (the numbers at the bottom of checks), your driver's license number, or another identification number. The merchant who rejects your check should give you its check verification company contact information so you can find out what information the thief is using. If you find that the thief is using your MICR code, ask your bank to close your checking account, and open a new one.

> *Tip:*
> *The merchant who rejects your check should give you its check verification company contact information so you can find out what information the thief is using.*

If you discover that the thief is using your driver's license number or some other identification number, work with your DMV or other identification issuing agency to get new identification with new numbers. Once you have taken the appropriate steps, your checks should be accepted.

The check verification company may or may not remove the information about the MICR code or the driver's license/identification number from its database because this information may help prevent the thief from continuing to commit fraud.

Also, if the checks are being passed on a new account, contact the bank to close the account. Also contact Chex Systems, Inc., to review your consumer report to make sure that no other bank accounts have been opened in your name.

Lastly, be sure to dispute any bad checks passed in your name with merchants so they don't start any collections actions against you.

> *Tip:*
> *Be sure to dispute any bad checks passed in your name with merchants so they don't start any collections actions against you.*

Fraudulent New Accounts

If you have trouble opening a new checking account, it may be because an identity thief has been opening accounts in your name. Chex Systems, Inc., produces consumer reports specifically about checking accounts, and as a consumer reporting company, is subject to the Fair Credit Reporting Act. You can request a free copy of your consumer report by contacting Chex Systems, Inc. If you find inaccurate information on your consumer report, follow the procedures identified elsewhere in this guide for correcting credit reports to dispute it. Contact each of the banks where account inquiries were made, too. This will help ensure that any fraudulently opened accounts are closed.

Contact Chex Systems at:
1-800-428-9623
www.chexhelp.com
Fax: 602-659-2197

Chex Systems, Inc.
Attn: Consumer Relations
7805 Hudson Road, Suite 100
Woodbury, MN 55125

Bankruptcy Fraud

If you believe someone has filed for bankruptcy in your name, write to the U.S. Trustee in the region where the bankruptcy was filed. A list of the U.S. Trustee Programs' Regional Offices is available on the UST website (www.usdoj.gov/ust), or check the Blue Pages of your phone book under U.S. Government Bankruptcy Administration.

In your letter, describe the situation and provide proof of your identity. The U.S. Trustee will make a criminal referral to law enforcement authorities if you provide appropriate documentation to substantiate your claim. You also may want to file a complaint with the U.S. Attorney and/or the FBI in the city where the bankruptcy was filed. The U.S. Trustee does not provide legal representation, legal advice, or referrals to lawyers. That means you may need to hire an attorney to help convince the bankruptcy court that the filing is fraudulent. When you or your attorney ask the bankruptcy court to dismiss the fraudulently filed bankruptcy case, you also should request that the bankruptcy court include in its order of dismissal facts that will help you repair your credit, including a statement that you did not file this bankruptcy case and that the case was filed by an imposter as the result of identity theft. Ask the bankruptcy court to send a copy of the dismissal order to each consumer reporting company; if the court will not do so, you should send the order to the consumer reporting companies yourself. Some courts will even provide you with several official copies of the order at no charge so that you can send them to creditors or use them in case of future problems. The U.S. Trustee does not provide consumers with copies of court documents. You can get them from the bankruptcy clerk's office for a fee.

When Financial Institutions are Uncooperative

If you have trouble getting a financial institution to help you resolve your banking-related identity theft problems, including problems with bank-issued credit cards, contact the agency that oversees your bank, such as the FDIC.

If you're not sure which of these agencies is the right one, visit the National Information Center of the Federal Reserve System at:

www.ffiec.gov/nicpubweb/nicweb/nichome.aspx and click on "Institution Search."

Federal Deposit Insurance Corporation - The FDIC supervises state-chartered banks that are not members of the Federal Reserve System, and insures deposits at banks and savings and loans. Call the FDIC Consumer Call Center toll-free: 1-800-934-3342; or write: Federal Deposit Insurance Corporation, Division of Compliance and Consumer Affairs, 550 17th Street, NW, Washington, DC 20429.

Federal Reserve System - The Fed supervises state-chartered banks that are members of the Federal Reserve

System. Call: 202-452-3693; or write: Division of Consumer and Community Affairs, Mail Stop 801, Federal Reserve Board, Washington, DC 20551; or contact the Federal Reserve Bank in your area. The Reserve Banks are located in Boston, New York, Philadelphia, Cleveland, Richmond, Atlanta, Chicago, St. Louis, Minneapolis, Kansas City, Dallas, and San Francisco.

National Credit Union Administration - The NCUA charters and supervises federal credit unions and insures deposits at federal credit unions and many state credit unions. Call: 703-518-6360; or write: Compliance Officer, National Credit Union Administration, 1775 Duke Street, Alexandria, VA 22314.

Office of the Comptroller of Currency - The OCC charters and supervises national banks. If the word "national" appears in the name of a bank, or the initials "N.A." follow its name, the OCC oversees its operations. Call toll-free: 1-800-613-6743 (business days 9:00 a.m. to 4:00 p.m. CST); fax: 713-336-4301; or write: Customer Assistance Group, 1301 McKinney Street, Suite 3710, Houston, TX 77010.

Office of Thrift Supervision - The OTS is the primary regulator of all federal, and many state-chartered, thrift institutions, including savings banks and savings and loan institutions. Call: 202-906-6000; or write: Office of Thrift Supervision, 1700 G Street, NW, Washington, DC 20552

Correcting Credit Reports

The Fair Credit Reporting Act (FCRA) establishes procedures for correcting fraudulent information on your credit report and requires that your report be made available only for certain legitimate business needs.

Everything You Need to Know About Identity Theft

Under the FCRA, both the consumer reporting company and the information provider (the business that sent the information to the consumer reporting company), such as a bank or credit card company, are responsible for correcting fraudulent information in your report. To protect your rights under the law, contact both the consumer reporting company and the information provider.

Consumer reporting companies will block fraudulent information from appearing on your credit report if you take the following steps: Send them a copy of an identity theft report and a letter telling them what information is fraudulent. The letter also should state that the information does not relate to any transaction that you made or authorized. In addition, provide proof of your identity that may include your SSN, name, address, and other personal information requested by the consumer reporting company.

The consumer reporting company has four business days to block the fraudulent information after accepting your identity theft report. It also must tell the information provider that it has blocked the information. The consumer reporting company may refuse to block the information or remove the block if, for example, you have not told the truth about your identity theft. If the consumer reporting company removes the block or refuses to place the block, it must let you know.

The blocking process is only one way for identity theft victims to deal with fraudulent information. There is also the "reinvestigation process," which was designed to help all consumers dispute errors or inaccuracies on their credit reports.

Information providers stop reporting fraudulent information to the consumer reporting companies once you send them an identity theft report and a letter explaining that the information they're reporting resulted from identity theft. But you must send your identity theft report and letter to the address specified by the information provider. Note that the information provider may continue to report the information if it later learns that the information does not result from identity theft.

If a consumer reporting company tells an information provider that it has blocked fraudulent information in your credit report, the information provider may not continue to report that information to the consumer reporting company. The information provider also may not hire someone to collect the debt that relates to the fraudulent account, or sell that debt to anyone else who would try to collect it.

Credit Card Problems

The Fair Credit Billing Act (FCBA) and the Electronic Fund Transfer Act (EFTA) offer procedures for you to use if your cards are lost or stolen.

Report the loss or theft of your credit cards and your ATM or debit cards to the card issuers as quickly as possible. Many companies have toll-free numbers and 24-hour service to deal with such emergencies. It's a good idea to follow up your phone calls with a letter. Include your account number, when you noticed your card was missing, and the date you first reported the loss.

Tip:
You also may want to check your homeowner's insurance policy to see if it covers your liability for card thefts.

You also may want to check your homeowner's insurance policy to see if it covers your liability for card thefts. If not, some insurance companies will allow you to change your policy to include this protection.

Your maximum liability under federal law for unauthorized use of your credit card is $50. If you report the loss before your credit cards are used, the FCBA says the card issuer cannot hold you responsible for any unauthorized charges. If a thief uses your cards before you report them missing, the most you will owe for unauthorized charges is $50 per card. Also, if the loss involves your credit card number, but not the card itself, you have no liability for unauthorized use.

After the loss, review your billing statements carefully. If they show any unauthorized charges, it's best to send a letter to the card issuer describing each questionable charge. Again, tell the card issuer the date your card was lost or stolen, or when you first noticed unauthorized charges, and when you first reported the problem to them. Be sure to send the letter to the address provided for billing errors. Do not send it with a payment or to the address where you send your payments unless you are directed to do so.

Your liability under federal law for unauthorized use of your ATM or debit card depends on how quickly you report the loss. If you report an ATM or debit card missing before it's used without your permission, the EFTA says the card issuer cannot hold you responsible for any unauthorized transfers. If unauthorized use occurs before you report it, your liability under federal law depends on how quickly you report the loss.

> *Tip:*
> *Your liability under federal law for unauthorized use of your ATM or debit card depends on how quickly you report the loss.*

For example, if you report the loss within two business days after you realize your card is missing, you will not be responsible for more than $50 for unauthorized use. However, if you don't report the loss within two business days after you discover the loss, you could lose up to $500 because of an unauthorized transfer. You also risk unlimited loss if you fail to report an unauthorized transfer within 60 days after your bank statement containing unauthorized use is mailed to you. That means you could lose all the money in your bank account and the unused portion of your line of credit established for overdrafts. However, for unauthorized transfers involving only your debit card number (not the loss of the card), you are liable only for transfers that occur after 60 days following the mailing of your bank statement containing the unauthorized use and before you report the loss.

You should send your letter by certified mail, and request a return receipt. It becomes your proof of the date the creditor received the letter. Include copies (NOT originals) of your police report or other documents that support your position. Keep a copy of your dispute letter.

The creditor must acknowledge your complaint in writing within 30 days after receiving it, unless the problem has been resolved. The creditor must resolve the dispute within two billing cycles (but not more than 90 days) after receiving your letter.

Criminal Violations

Procedures to correct your record within criminal justice databases can vary from state to state, and even from county to county. Some states have enacted laws with special procedures for identity theft victims to follow to clear their names. You should check with the office of your state Attorney General, but you can use the following information as a general guide.

If wrongful criminal violations are attributed to your name, contact the police or sheriff's department that originally arrested the person using your identity, or the court agency that issued the warrant for the arrest. File an impersonation report with the police/sheriff's department or the court, and confirm your identity: Ask the police department to take a full set of your fingerprints, photograph you, and make copies of your photo identification documents, like your driver's license, passport, or travel visa. To establish your innocence, ask the police to compare the prints and photographs with those of the imposter.

If the arrest warrant is from a state or county other than where you live, ask your local police department to send the impersonation report to the police department in the jurisdiction where the arrest warrant, traffic citation, or criminal conviction originated.

The law enforcement agency should then recall any warrants and issue a "clearance letter" or "certificate of release" (if you were arrested/booked). You'll need to keep this document with you at all times in case you're wrongly arrested again. Ask the law enforcement agency to file the record of the follow-up investigation establishing your innocence with the district attorney's (D.A.) office and/or court where the crime took place. This will result in an amended complaint. Once your name is recorded in a criminal database, it is unlikely that it will be completely removed from the official record. Ask that the "key name" or "primary name" be changed from your name to the imposter's name (or to "John Doe" if the imposter's true identity is not known), with your name noted as an alias.

You'll also want to clear your name in the court records. To do so, you'll need to determine which state law(s) will help you with this and how. If your state has no formal procedure for clearing your record, contact the D.A.'s office in the county where the case was originally prosecuted. Ask the D.A.'s office for the appropriate court records needed to clear your name. You may need to hire a criminal defense attorney to help you clear your name. Contact Legal Services in your state or your local bar association for help in finding an attorney.

Finally, contact your state Department of Motor Vehicles (DMV) to find out if your driver's license is being used by the identity thief. Ask that your files be flagged for possible fraud.

Debt Collectors

The Fair Debt Collection Practices Act prohibits debt collectors from using unfair or deceptive practices to collect overdue bills that a creditor has forwarded for collection, even if those bills don't result from identity theft.

You can stop a debt collector from contacting you in two ways:

- Write a letter to the collection agency telling them to stop. Once the debt collector receives your letter, the company may not contact you again — with two exceptions: They can tell you there will be no further contact, and they can tell you that the debt collector or the creditor intends to take some specific action.

> *Tip:*
> If the debt you're disputing originates from a credit card you never applied for ask for a copy of the application with the applicant's signature.

- Send a letter to the collection agency, within 30 days after you received written notice of the debt, telling them that you do not owe the money. Include copies of documents that support your position. Including a copy (NOT original) of your police report may be useful. In this case, a collector can renew collection activities only if it sends you proof of the debt.

If you don't have documentation to support your position, be as specific as possible about why the debt collector is mistaken. The debt collector is responsible for sending you proof that you're wrong. For example, if the debt you're disputing originates from a credit card you never applied for ask for a copy of the application with the applicant's signature. Then, you can prove that it's not your signature.

If you tell the debt collector that you are a victim of identity theft and it is collecting the debt for another company, the debt collector must tell that company that you may be a victim of identity theft.

While you can stop a debt collector from contacting you, that won't get rid of the debt itself. To dispute the debt, it's important to contact the company that originally opened the account, otherwise that company may send it to a different debt collector, report it on your credit report, or initiate a lawsuit to collect on the debt.

Your Driver's License

If you think your name or SSN is being used by an identity thief to get a driver's license or a non-driver's ID card, contact your state Department of Motor Vehicles. If your state uses your SSN as your driver's license number, ask to substitute another number.

> *Tip:*
> *If your state uses your SSN as your driver's license number, ask to substitute another number.*

If you think your name or SSN is being used by an identity thief to get a driver's license or a non-driver's ID card, contact your state DMV. If your state uses your SSN as your driver's license number, ask to substitute another number.

Investment Fraud

The United States Securities and Exchange Commission's Office of Investor Education and Assistance serves investors who complain to the SEC about investment fraud or the mishandling of their investments by securities professionals. If you believe that an identity thief has tampered with your securities investments or a brokerage account, immediately report it to your broker or account manager and to the SEC. You can file a complaint with the SEC's Complaint Center at www.sec.gov/complaint.shtml. Include as much detail as possible. If you do not have Internet access, write to the SEC at: SEC Office of Investor Education and Assistance, 100 F Street, NE, Washington, DC 20549. For answers to general questions, call 202-551-6551.

Mail Fraud

The United State Postal Inspection Service (USPIS) is the law enforcement arm of the U.S. Postal Service, and investigates cases of identity theft. The USPIS has primary jurisdiction in all matters infringing on the integrity of the U.S. mail. If an identity thief has stolen your mail to get new credit cards, bank or credit card statements, pre-screened credit offers, or tax information, or has falsified change-of-address forms or obtained your personal information through a fraud conducted by mail, report it to your local postal inspector.

You can locate the USPIS district office nearest you by calling your local post office, checking the Blue Pages of your telephone directory, or visiting:

www.usps.gov/websites/depart/inspect.

Passport Fraud

If you've lost your passport, or believe it was stolen or is being used fraudulently, contact the United States Department of State through its website, or call a local USDS field office. Local field offices are listed in the Blue Pages of your telephone directory.

www.travel.state.gov/passport/passport_1738.html

Telephone Fraud

If an identity thief has established phone service in your name, is making unauthorized calls that seem to come from – and are billed to – your cellular phone, or is using your calling card and PIN, contact your service provider immediately to cancel the account and/or calling card. Open new accounts and choose new PINs. If you're having trouble getting fraudulent phone charges removed from your account or getting an unauthorized account closed, contact the appropriate agency below.

- For local service, contact your state Public Utility Commission.
- For cellular phones and long distance, contact the Federal Communications Commission (FCC) at www.fcc.gov. The FCC regulates interstate and international communications by radio, television, wire, satellite, and cable. Call: 1-888-CALL-FCC; TTY: 1-888-TELL-FCC; or write: Federal Communications Commission, Consumer Information Bureau, 445 12th Street, SW, Room 5A863, Washington, DC 20554. You can file complaints online at www.fcc.gov, or e-mail your questions to fccinfo@fcc.gov.

Social Security Number Fraud and Misuse

If you have specific information of SSN misuse that involves the buying or selling of Social Security cards, may be related to terrorist activity, or is designed to obtain Social Security benefits, contact the SSA Office of the Inspector General. You may file a complaint online at www.socialsecurity.gov/oig, call toll-free: 1-800-269-0271, fax: 410-597-0118, or write: SSA Fraud Hotline, P.O. Box 17768, Baltimore, MD 21235.

You also may call SSA toll-free at 1-800-772-1213 to verify the accuracy of the earnings reported on your SSN, request a copy of your Social Security Statement, or get a replacement SSN card if yours is lost or stolen. Follow up in writing.

Student Loans

Contact the school or program that opened the student loan to close the loan. At the same time, report the fraudulent loan to the U.S. Department of Education. Call the Inspector General's Hotline toll-free at 1-800-MIS-USED; visit www.ed.gov/about/offices/list/oig/hotline.html?src=rt; or write: Office of Inspector General, U.S. Department of Education, 400 Maryland Avenue, SW, Washington, DC 20202-1510.

Tax Fraud

The Internal Revenue Service (IRS) is responsible for administering and enforcing tax laws. Identity fraud may occur as it relates directly to your tax records. Visit www.irs.gov and type in the IRS key word "Identity Theft" for more information.

If you have an unresolved issue related to identity theft, or you have suffered or are about to suffer a significant hardship as a result of the administration of the tax laws, visit the IRS Taxpayer Advocate Service website www.irs.gov/advocate/ or call toll-free: 1-877-777-4778.

Medical Identity Theft

Could identity thieves be using your personal and health insurance information to get medical treatment, prescription drugs or surgery? Could dishonest people working in a medical setting be using your information to submit false bills to insurance companies? Medical identity theft is a twist on traditional identity theft. Like traditional identity theft, medical ID theft can affect your finances; but it also can take a toll on your health.

You may be a victim of medical identity theft if:

- you get a bill for medical services you didn't receive;
- a debt collector contacts you about medical debt you don't owe;
- you order a copy of your credit report and see medical collection notices you don't recognize;
- you try to make a legitimate insurance claim and your health plan says you've reached your limit on benefits; or
- you are denied insurance because your medical records show a condition you don't have.

Medical identity theft may change your medical and health insurance records: Every time a thief uses your identity to get care, a record is created with the imposter's medical information that could be mistaken for your medical information — say, a different blood type, an inaccurate history of drug or alcohol abuse, test results that aren't yours, or a diagnosis of an illness, allergy or condition you don't have. Any of these could lead to improper treatment, which in turn, could lead to injury, illness or worse.

Preventing Medical Identity Theft

While there's no fool-proof way to avoid medical identity theft, the FTC says you can take a few steps to minimize your risk.

Verify a source before sharing information. Don't give out personal or medical information on the phone or through the mail unless you've initiated the contact and you're sure you know who you're dealing with. Be wary of offers of "free" health services or products from providers who require you to give them your health plan ID number. Medical identity thieves may pose as employees of insurance companies, doctors' offices, clinics, pharmacies, and even government agencies to get people to reveal their personal information. Then, they use it to commit fraud, like submitting false claims for Medicare reimbursement.

Safeguard your medical and health insurance information. If you keep copies of your medical or health insurance records, make sure they're secure, whether they're on paper in a desk drawer or electronic in a file online. Be on guard when you use the Internet, especially to access accounts or records related to your medical care or insurance. If you are asked to share sensitive personal information like your Social Security number, insurance account information or any details of your health or medical conditions on the Internet, ask why it's needed, how it will be kept safe, and whether it

> *Tip:*
> *Medical identity thieves may pose as employees of insurance companies, doctors' offices, clinics, pharmacies, and even government agencies to get people to reveal their personal information.*

will be shared. Look for website privacy policies and read them: They should specify how site operators maintain the accuracy of the personal information they collect, as well as how they secure it, who has access to it, how they will use the information you provide, and whether they will share it with third parties. If you decide to share your information online, look for indicators that the site is secure, like a lock icon on the browser's status bar or a URL that begins "https:" (the "s" is for secure). Remember that email is not secure.

Treat your trash carefully. To thwart a medical identity thief who may pick through your trash or recycling bins to capture your personal and medical information, shred your health insurance forms and prescription and physician statements. It's also a good idea to destroy the labels on your prescription bottles and packages before you throw them out.

Detecting Medical Identity Theft

Read the Explanation of Benefits (EOB) statement that your health plan sends you after treatment. If you are a Medicare beneficiary, read the Medicare Summary Notice. Make sure the claims paid match the care you received. Look for the name of the provider, the date of service, and the service provided. If there's a discrepancy, contact your health plan to report the problem.

> *Tip:*
> *Read the Explanation of Benefits (EOB) statement that your health plan sends you after treatment.*

Order a copy of your credit reports, and review them carefully. Once you have your reports, look for inquiries from companies you didn't contact, accounts you didn't open, and debts on your accounts that you can't explain. Check that your Social Security number, your address (es), name or initials, and your employers are listed correctly. If you find inaccurate or fraudulent information, get it fixed or removed.

Ask for a copy of your medical records. If you believe you've already been a victim of medical identity theft, review your medical and health insurance records regularly. The thief may have used your name to see a doctor, get prescription drugs with your health ID number, file claims with your insurance provider, or done other things that leave a trail in your medical records. Try to review your health records for inaccuracies before you seek additional medical care. The Health Insurance Portability and Accountability Act (HIPAA) Privacy Rule gives you the right to copies of your records that are maintained by health plans and medical providers covered by that law. Health care providers and health plans generally are required to give you your files within 30 days after you ask for them. Unlike credit reports, there is no central source for your medical records. You need to contact each provider you do business with – including doctors, clinics, hospitals, pharmacies, laboratories and health plans – that is relevant to your experience. For example, if a thief got a prescription in your name, you may want the record from the pharmacy that filled the prescription and the health care provider who wrote the prescription. Or if you've been using the same hospital for 20 years and you think that the identity theft is recent, you may want to limit your request to records of the last few years or months.

It's likely that you have to complete a form and pay a fee to get a copy of your records. Keep track of your communications with your health plan and providers, including copies of postal and email correspondence, and a log of your phone calls, conversations and activities. Be patient: Health plans and providers, particularly small ones, may not have handled a claim of medical identity theft before, and may not be sure how to respond.

In most instances, a provider who denies you access to your records must give you the reason in writing. Some providers may refuse to give you copies of your medical or billing records for fear that they're violating the identity thief's HIPAA privacy rights. These providers are mistaken: You have the right to know what's in your file. If your request is denied, you have the right to appeal. Contact the person identified in the provider's Notice of Privacy Practices or the patient representative or ombudsman, explain the situation and request your file. If a provider still refuses to give you access to your records within 30 days of your written request, file a complaint with the U.S. Department of Health and Human Services' Office for Civil Rights, at www.hhs.gov/ocr.

You also should get a copy of the accounting of disclosures for your medical record from your health plan and providers. It will help you follow the trail of your information and identify who has incorrect information about you. The law allows you to order one free copy of the accounting from each of your providers every 12 months. The accounting is a record of:

- the date of the disclosure;
- the name of the person or entity who received the information;
- a brief description of the information disclosed;
- a brief statement of the purpose of the disclosure or a copy of the request for it.

Certain disclosures that occur often or as a matter of routine – like each time a doctor's office sends treatment information to another health care provider, or sends payment information to an insurer for reimbursement – may not be included in the accounting.

In addition to other steps outlined in this guide, you should also exercise your right under HIPAA to correct errors in your medical and billing records. Write to your health plan or provider detailing the information that seems inaccurate. Include copies (keep the originals) of any document that supports your position. In addition to providing your complete name and address, your letter should identify each item in your record that you dispute, state the facts and your reasons for disputing the information, and request that each error be corrected or deleted. You may want to enclose a copy of your medical record with the items in question circled. Send your letter by certified mail, and ask for a "return receipt," so you can document what the plan or provider received. Keep copies of your dispute letter and enclosures.

> **Tip:**
> *You should also exercise your right under HIPAA to correct errors in your medical and billing records.*

Generally, your health plan or medical provider must respond: The creator of the information is obligated to amend the inaccurate or incomplete information. It also should notify other parties, like labs or other health care providers that may have received incorrect information. If an investigation doesn't resolve your dispute with your plan or provider, you can ask that a statement of the dispute be included in your record.

5

Ongoing Vigilance

Once resolved, most cases of identity theft stay resolved. But occasionally, some victims have recurring problems. To help stay on top of the situation, continue to monitor your credit reports and read your financial account statements promptly and carefully. You may want to review your credit reports once every three months in the first year of the theft, and once a year thereafter. And stay alert for other signs of identity theft, like:

- failing to receive bills or other mail. Follow up with creditors if your bills don't arrive on time. A missing bill could mean an identity thief has taken over your account and changed your billing address to cover his tracks.
- receiving credit cards that you didn't apply for.

- being denied credit, or being offered less favorable credit terms, like a high interest rate, for no apparent reason.
- getting calls or letters from debt collectors or businesses about merchandise or services you didn't buy.

Get Your Credit Reports

The Fair Credit Reporting Act requires each of the nationwide consumer re- porting companies — Equifax, Experian, and TransUnion — to provide you with a free copy of your credit report, at your request, once every 12 months.

Fact:
You are entitled to a free copy of your credit report, at your request, once every 12 months.

To order your free annual report from one or all the national consumer reporting companies, visit www.annualcreditreport.com, call toll-free 1-877-322-8228, or complete the Annual Credit Report Request Form and mail it to: Annual Credit Report Request Service, P.O. Box 105281, Atlanta, GA 30348-5281. Do not contact the three nationwide consumer reporting companies individually. They provide free annual credit reports only through www.annualcreditreport.com, 1-877-322-8228, and Annual Credit Report Request Service, P.O. Box 105281, Atlanta, GA 30348-5281.

The FTC advises consumers who order their free annual credit reports online to be sure to correctly spell www.annualcreditreport.com, or link to it from the FTC's website to avoid being misdirected to other websites that offer supposedly free reports, but only with the purchase of other products. While consumers may be offered additional products or services while on the authorized website, they are not required to make a purchase to receive their free annual credit reports.

Additional Reports

Under federal law, you're entitled to a free report if a company takes adverse action against you, such as denying your application for credit, insurance, or employment, and you request your report within 60 days of receiving notice of the action. The notice will give you the name, address, and phone number of the consumer reporting company. You're also entitled to one free report a year if you're unemployed and plan to look for a job within 60 days; you're on welfare; or your report is inaccurate because of fraud. Otherwise, a consumer reporting company may charge you up to $10.50 for another copy of your report within a 12-month period.

To buy a copy of your report, contact:

- Equifax: 1-800-685-1111; www.equifax.com
- Experian: 1-888-EXPERIAN (1-888-397-3742); www.experian.com
- Transunion: 1-800-916-8800; www.transunion.com

Under state law, consumers in Colorado, Georgia, Maine, Maryland, Massachusetts, New Jersey, and Vermont already have free access to their credit reports.

Active Alerts for Military Personnel

If you are a member of the military and away from your usual duty station, you may place an active duty alert on your credit reports to help minimize the risk of identity theft while you are deployed. Active duty alerts are in effect on your report for one year. If your deployment lasts longer, you can place another alert on your credit report.

When you place an active duty alert, you'll be removed from the credit reporting companies' marketing list for pre-screened credit card offers for two years unless you ask to go back on the list before then.

Prevention is Key

There are several things that everyone can do immediately to minimize identity theft and to prevent recurrence if you have been a victim.

Place passwords on your credit card, bank, and phone accounts. Avoid using easily available information like your mother's maiden name, your birth date, the last four digits of your SSN or your phone number, or a series of consecutive numbers. When opening new accounts, you may find that many businesses still have a line on their applications for your mother's maiden name. Ask if you can use a password instead.

Secure personal information in your home, especially if you have roommates, employ outside help, or are having work done in your home.

Ask about information security procedures in your workplace or at businesses, doctor's offices, or other institutions that collect your personally identifying information. Find out who has access to your personal information and verify that it is handled securely. Ask about the disposal procedures for those records as well. Find out if your information will be shared with anyone else. If so, ask how your information can be kept confidential

Guard Your Personal Information

Don't give out personal information on the phone, through the mail, or on the Internet unless you've initiated the contact or are sure you know who you're dealing with. Identity thieves are clever, and have posed as representatives of banks, Internet service providers (ISPs), and even government agencies to get people to reveal their SSN, mother's maiden name, account numbers, and other identifying information. Before you share any personal information, confirm that you are dealing with a legitimate organization. Check an organization's website by typing its URL in the address line, rather than cutting and pasting it. Many companies post scam alerts when their name is used improperly.

Don't carry your SSN card; leave it in a secure place.

Give your SSN only when absolutely necessary, and ask to use other types of identifiers. If your state uses your SSN as your driver's license number, ask to substitute another number. Do the same if your health insurance company uses your SSN as your policy number.

Before you reveal any personally identifying information, find out how it will be used and whether it will be shared with others. Ask about company's privacy policy: Will you have a choice about the use of your information; can you choose to have it kept confidential?

Put passwords on your all your accounts, including your credit card account, and your bank and phone accounts. Avoid using easily available information — like your mother's maiden name, your birth date, the last four digits of your SSN, or your phone number — or obvious choices, like a series of consecutive numbers or your hometown football team.

Keep items with personal information in a safe place. When you discard receipts, copies of credit applications, insurance forms, physician statements, bank checks and statements, expired charge cards, credit offers you get in the mail, and mailing labels from magazines, tear or shred them. That will help thwart any identity thief who may pick through your trash or recycling bins to capture your personal information.

Guard Your Mail and Trash

Deposit your outgoing mail in post office collection boxes or at your local post office, rather than in an unsecured mailbox. Promptly remove mail from your mailbox. If you're planning to be away from home and can't pick up your mail, call the U.S. Postal Service at 1-800-275-8777 to request a vacation hold. The Postal Service will hold your mail at your local post office until you can pick it up or are home to receive it.

To thwart an identity thief who may pick through your trash or recycling bins to capture your personal information, tear or shred your charge receipts, copies of credit applications, insurance forms, physician statements, checks and bank statements, expired charge cards that you're discarding, and credit offers you get in the mail. To opt out of receiving offers of credit in the mail, call: 1-888-5-OPTOUT (1-888-567-8688). The three nationwide consumer reporting companies use the same toll-free number to let consumers choose not to receive credit offers based on their lists. Be aware, however, that you will be asked to provide your SSN which the consumer reporting companies need to match you with your file.

Tip:
To opt out of receiving offers of credit in the mail, call: 1-888-5-OPTOUT (1-888-567-8688).

Your Personal Belongings

Carry only the identification information and the credit and debit cards that you'll actually need when you go out.

Be cautious when responding to promotions. Identity thieves may create phony promotional offers to get you to give them your personal information.

Keep your purse or wallet in a safe place at work; do the same with copies of administrative forms that have your sensitive personal information. Minimize the identification information and the number of cards you carry to what you'll actually need. Don't put all your identifying information in one holder in your purse, briefcase, or backpack.

When ordering new checks, pick them up from the bank instead of having them mailed to your home.

Sharing Your Social Security Number

Your employer and financial institutions will need your SSN for wage and tax reporting purposes. other businesses may ask you for your SSN to do a credit check if you are applying for a loan, renting an apartment, or signing up for utilities. Sometimes, however, they simply want your SSN for general record keeping. If someone asks for your SSN, ask:

> **Fact:**
> Many states restrict businesses from using your SSN as an identifying number.

- Why do you need my SSN?
- How will it be used?
- How do you protect it from being stolen?

If you don't provide your SSN, some businesses may not provide you with the service or benefit you want. Getting satisfactory answers to these questions will help you decide whether you want to share your SSN with the business. The decision to share is yours.

You should also know that many states restrict the use of a SSN as an identifying number and it may actually be illegal for the business to request it of you.

Protecting Your Credit, ATM and Debit Cards

The best protections against card fraud are to know where your cards are at all times and to keep them secure. For protection of ATM and debit cards that involve a Personal Identification Number (PIN), keep your PIN a secret. Don't use your address, birthdate, phone or Social Security number as the PIN and do memorize the number.

For Credit and ATM or Debit Cards:

- Be cautious about disclosing your account number over the phone unless you know you're dealing with a reputable company.
- Never put your account number on the outside of an envelope or on a postcard.
- Draw a line through blank spaces on charge or debit slips above the total so the amount cannot be changed.
- Don't sign a blank charge or debit slip.
- Tear up carbons and save your receipts to check against your monthly statements.
- Cut up old cards - cutting through the account number - before disposing of them.
- Open monthly statements promptly and compare them with your receipts. Report mistakes or discrepancies as soon as possible to the special address listed on your statement for inquiries. Under

> *Tip:*
> Keep a record - in a safe place separate from your cards - of your account numbers, expiration dates, and the telephone numbers of each card issuer so you can report a loss quickly.

the FCBA (credit cards) and the EFTA (ATM or debit cards), the card issuer must investigate errors reported to them within 60 days of the date your statement was mailed to you.
- Keep a record - in a safe place separate from your cards - of your account numbers, expiration dates, and the telephone numbers of each card issuer so you can report a loss quickly.
- Carry only those cards that you anticipate you'll need.

For ATM or debit cards:

- Don't carry your PIN in your wallet or purse or write it on your ATM or debit card.
- Never write your PIN on the outside of a deposit slip, an envelope, or other papers that could be easily lost or seen.
- Carefully check ATM or debit card transactions before you enter the PIN or before you sign the receipt; the funds for this item will be fairly quickly transferred out of your checking or other deposit account.
- Periodically check your account activity. This is particularly important if you bank online. Compare the current balance and recent withdrawals or transfers to those you've recorded, including your current ATM and debit card withdrawals and purchases and your recent checks. If you notice transactions you didn't make, or if your balance has dropped suddenly without activity by you, immediately report the problem to your card issuer. Someone may have co-opted your account information to commit fraud.

Everything You Need to Know About Identity Theft

Computers and the Internet

You may be careful about locking your doors and windows, and keeping your personal papers in a secure place. Depending on what you use your personal computer for, an identity thief may not need to set foot in your house to steal your personal information. You may store your SSN, financial records, tax returns, birth date, and bank account numbers on your computer. These tips can help you keep your computer – and the personal information it stores – safe.

Virus protection software should be updated regularly, and patches for your operating system and other software programs should be installed to protect against intrusions and infections that can lead to the compromise of your computer files or passwords. Ideally, virus protection software should be set to automatically update each week. The Windows operating system also can be set to automatically check for patches and download them to your computer.

Do not open files sent to you by strangers, or click on hyperlinks or download programs from people you don't know. Be careful about using file-sharing programs. Opening a file could expose your system to a computer virus or a program known as "spyware," which could capture your passwords or any other information as you type it into your keyboard.

Tip: Do not open files sent to you by strangers, or click on hyperlinks or download programs from people you don't know

Use a firewall program, especially if you use a high-speed Internet connection like cable, DSL or T-1 that leaves your computer connected to the Internet 24 hours a day. The firewall program will allow you to stop uninvited access to your computer. Without it, hackers can take over your computer, access the personal information stored on it, or use it to commit other crimes.

Use a secure browser – software that encrypts or scrambles information you send over the Internet – to guard your online transactions. Be sure your browser has the most up-to-date encryption capabilities by using the latest version available from the manufacturer. You also can download some browsers for free over the Internet. When submitting information, look for the "lock" icon on the browser's status bar to be sure your information is secure during transmission.

Try not to store financial information on your laptop unless absolutely necessary. If you do, use a strong password – a combination of letters (upper and lower case), numbers, and symbols. A good way to create a strong password is to think of a memorable phrase and use the first letter of each word as your password, converting some letters into numbers that resemble letters. For example, "I love Felix; he's a good cat," would become 1LFHA6c. Don't use an automatic log-in feature that saves your user name and password, and always log off when you're finished. That way, if your laptop is stolen, it's harder for a thief to access your personal information.

Before you dispose of a computer, delete all the personal information it stored. Deleting files using the keyboard or mouse commands or reformatting your hard drive may not be enough because the files may stay on the computer's hard drive, where they may be retrieved easily. Use a "wipe" utility program to overwrite the entire hard drive.

Look for website privacy policies. They should answer questions about maintaining accuracy, access, security, and control of personal information collected by the site, how the information will be used, and whether it will be provided to third parties. If you don't see a privacy policy, or if you can't understand it, consider doing business elsewhere.

Using Public Wireless Networks

Public wireless networks such as those Wi-Fi hotspots in coffee shops, libraries, airports, hotels, universities, and other public places, allow people to access the internet through a shared network. While convenient, they're often not secure. You are sharing the network with strangers, and some of them may be interested in your personal information.

Encryption is the key to keeping your personal information secure online. Encryption scrambles the information you send over the internet into a code so that it's not accessed by others. When using wireless networks, it's best to send personal information only if it's encrypted — either by an encrypted website or a secure network. An encrypted website protects only the information you send to and from that site. A secure wireless network encrypts all of the information you send while online.

If you send email, share digital photos and videos, use online tools to manage calendars and contact lists, use social networks, or bank online, you're sending personal information over the internet. The information you share is stored on a server — a powerful computer that collects and delivers content. Many websites, such as banking sites, use encryption to protect your information as it travels from your computer to their server.

To determine if a website is encrypted, look for ***https*** at the beginning of the web address (the "s" is for secure), and a ***lock icon*** at the top or bottom of your browser window. The exact position of the lock depends on which browser you use. Some websites use encryption only on the sign-in page, but if any part of your session isn't encrypted, the entire account could be vulnerable. Look for https and the lock icon the entire time you're on the site, not just when you sign in. You can also click on the lock icon to display information about the site and help you verify that it's not a fraudulent website.

Also note the following:

- If a hotspot doesn't require a password, it's not secure.
- If a hotspot asks for a password through your browser simply to grant access, or it asks for a WEP password, it's best to treat it as if it were unsecured.
- You can be confident a hotspot is secure only if you are asked to provide a WPA password. If you're not sure, the information you enter could be at risk. WPA2 is the most secure.

Most Wi-Fi hotspots don't encrypt the information you send over the internet and are *not* secure. If you use an unsecured network to log in to an unencrypted site — or a site that uses

> *Tip:*
> *If a hotspot doesn't require a password, it's not secure.*

encryption only on the sign-in page — other users on the network can see what you see and what you send. They could hijack your session and log in as you. Hacking tools make this easy, even for users with limited technical know-how. Your personal information, private documents, contacts, family photos, and even your login credentials could be up for grabs. An imposter could use your account to impersonate you and scam people you care about. In addition, an attacker could test your username and password to try to gain access to other websites — including sites that store your financial information.

Tips for protecting your information include:

- When using a Wi-Fi hotspot, only log in or send personal information to websites that you know are fully encrypted. And keep in mind that your entire visit to each site should be encrypted – from the time you log in to the site until you log out. If you think you're logged in to an encrypted site but find yourself on an unencrypted page, log out right away.
- Don't stay permanently signed in to accounts. When you've finished using an account, log out.
- Do not use the same password on different websites. It could give someone who gains access to one of your accounts access to many of your accounts.
- Many web browsers alert users who try to visit fraudulent websites or download malicious programs. Pay attention to these warnings, and take the extra minute or so to keep your browser and security software up-to-date.

> *Tip:*
> *Do not use the same password on different websites. It could give someone who gains access to one of your accounts access to many of your accounts.*

- If you regularly access online accounts through Wi-Fi hotspots, use a virtual private network (VPN). VPNs encrypt traffic between your computer and the internet, even on unsecured networks. You can obtain a personal VPN account from a VPN service provider. In addition, some organizations create VPNs to provide secure, remote access for their employees.
- Some Wi-Fi networks use encryption: WEP and WPA are the most common. WPA encryption protects your information against common hacking programs. WEP may not. If you aren't certain that

you are on a WPA network, use the same precautions as on an unsecured network.
- Installing browser add-ons or plug-ins can help, too. For example, Force-TLS and HTTPS-Everywhere are free Firefox add-ons that force the browser to use encryption on popular websites that usually aren't encrypted. They don't protect you on all websites – look for https in the URL and the lock icon to know a site is secure.

Products and Services for Purchase

Many people find value and convenience in paying an outside party to help them exercise their rights and protect their information. At the same time, some rights and protections you have under federal or state laws can help you protect your identity and recover from identity theft at no cost. Knowing and understanding your rights can help you determine whether — or which — commercial products or services may be appropriate for you. These include Fraud Alerts, Credit Freezes and Identity Theft Protection Products

Fraud Alerts

A fraud alert is a signal placed in your credit report or credit file to warn potential creditors that they must use what the law calls "reasonable policies and procedures" to verify your identity before they issue credit in your name. Fraud alerts may be effective at stopping someone from opening new credit accounts in your name, but they may not prevent the misuse of your existing accounts.

Under the federal Fair Credit Reporting Act (FCRA), you may be entitled to two kinds of free fraud alerts: initial and extended.

You may ask a consumer reporting company to place an initial fraud alert on your credit report if you suspect you have been, or are about to be, a victim of identity theft. This may be appropriate after your wallet or another source of personal information is lost or stolen. An initial fraud alert is good for 90 days, and can be renewed when appropriate. To place an initial fraud alert, call the toll-free fraud number of any one of the three national consumer reporting companies. The company you call is required to contact the other two; they, in turn, will place an alert on their versions of your report. Expect to receive a confirmation from each of the companies.

When you place an initial fraud alert on your credit report, you're entitled to order one free credit report from each of the consumer reporting companies; if you ask, only the last four digits of your Social Security number will appear on your reports.

If you have been a victim of identity theft, you may ask for an extended alert, which stays on your credit report for seven years. To get an extended fraud alert placed on your report, you will need to contact one of the credit bureaus, and provide an Identity Theft Report, such as a police report or other report to a law enforcement agency, including a report to the FTC. If your credit report has an extended alert, potential creditors must contact you in person, or by phone or some other method you have provided before they can issue credit in your name. When you place an extended alert on your credit report, you're entitled to two free credit reports from each of the consumer reporting companies within 12 months. In addition, the consumer reporting companies must remove your name from marketing lists for pre-screened offers of credit for five years — unless you ask them to put your name back on the list.

Credit Freezes

A credit freeze allows you to restrict access to your credit report. If you place a freeze on your report, potential creditors and certain other people or businesses can't get access to it unless you lift the freeze temporarily or permanently. For more information about credit freezes, check with your state attorney general's office or visit www.naag.org.

Limiting access to your credit report makes it more difficult for identity thieves to open new accounts in your name. That's because most creditors will need to view a credit file before opening a new account; if they can't see the file, they may not extend the credit. Still, a credit freeze may not prevent the misuse of your existing accounts or certain other types of identity theft.

A credit freeze is different from a fraud alert in a number of ways. A freeze generally stops all access to your credit report, while a fraud alert permits creditors to get your report as long as they take steps to verify your identity. The availability of a credit freeze depends on state law or a consumer reporting company's policies; fraud alerts are federal rights intended for consumers who believe they may have been, or actually have been, victims of identity theft. And some states charge a fee for placing or removing a freeze, although it is free to place or remove a fraud alert.

> *Tip:*
> A credit freeze generally stops all access to your credit report, while a fraud alert permits creditors to get your report as long as they take steps to verify your identity.

Most states have laws that allow consumers to place a credit freeze with consumer reporting companies. In many of these states, any consumer can freeze their credit file;

in others, only identity theft victims can freeze their files. The cost of placing a credit freeze and the lead times vary. In many states, credit freezes are free for identity theft victims; other consumers typically are charged about $10 per credit reporting company. Contact your state attorney general for the particulars of your state's freeze laws. To place a freeze, contact each of the nationwide consumer reporting companies because a credit freeze placed at one company is not referred to the other companies. And be aware that the three major credit reporting companies have begun offering credit freezes directly to consumers — for a fee — regardless of whether their state has a freeze law.

Placing a credit freeze does not affect your credit score, keep you from getting your free annual credit report, or keep you from buying your credit report or score. It doesn't prevent you from opening a new account yourself, applying for a job, renting an apartment, or buying insurance, either. In these situations, the business usually needs to review your credit report. You can ask the consumer reporting company to lift your credit freeze temporarily, or remove it altogether. But the cost and lead times to lift or remove a freeze vary, so it's wise to check with your state authorities or with a consumer reporting company in advance if possible.

> *Fact:*
> Placing a credit freeze does not affect your credit score, keep you from getting your free annual credit report, or keep you from buying your credit report or score.

Identity Theft Protection Products and Services for Sale

Identity theft protection companies offer a range of products and services for sale. Some allow you to "lock," "flag," or "freeze" your credit reports. Often, the companies advertising these services simply are offering to place a fraud alert or credit freeze on your report. These services also may renew or update your alerts or freezes automatically, as long as you continue to pay. Under the law, initial fraud alerts and renewals are available for free if you have reason to believe you have been — or are about to be — a victim of identity theft.

Some companies, including consumer reporting companies, offer subscriptions to credit monitoring services. These services track your credit report, and generally send you an email alert reflecting recent activity, such as an inquiry or new account. Typically, the more frequent or more detailed the report, the more expensive the service.

Some companies offer services to help you rebuild your identity in the event of identity theft. Typically, these services operate by obtaining a limited power of attorney from you, which enables the company to act on your behalf when dealing with consumer reporting companies, creditors, or other information sources.

Many companies may offer additional services, including removing your name from mailing lists or pre-screened offers of credit or insurance, representing your legal interests, "guaranteeing" reimbursement in the event you experience a loss due to identity theft, or helping you track down whether your personal information has been exposed online. Before you agree to pay for any of these services, read the fine print. You can get some of them yourself at no cost: for example, if you decide you don't want to receive pre-screened offers of credit and insurance, you can opt out for five years or permanently by calling toll-free 1-888-5-OPTOUT (1-888-567-8688) or visiting www.optoutprescreen.com.

The FTC has a library of resources to help victims of identity theft report the crime and take steps to recover their identity. Visit www.ftc.gov/idtheft.

6

Completing an Identity Theft Affidavit

To make certain that you do not become responsible for any debts incurred by an identity thief, you must prove to each of the companies where accounts were opened in your name that you didn't create the debt. The ID Theft Affidavit was developed by a group of credit grantors, consumer advocates, and attorneys at the Federal Trade Commission (FTC) for this purpose. Importantly, this affidavit is only for use where a new account was opened in your name. If someone made unauthorized charges to an existing account, call the company for instructions.

> *Fact:*
> *The ID Theft Affidavit may be required by a company in order for you to obtain applications or other transaction records related to the theft of your identity.*

While many companies accept this affidavit, others require that you submit more or different forms. Before you send the affidavit, contact each company to find out if they accept it. If they do not accept the ID Theft Affidavit, ask them what information and/or documentation they require.

You may not need the ID Theft Affidavit to absolve you of debt resulting from identity theft if you obtain an Identity Theft Report. We suggest you consider obtaining an Identity Theft Report where a new account was opened in your name. An Identity Theft Report can be used to (1) permanently block fraudulent information from appearing on your credit report; (2) ensure that debts do not reappear on your credit reports; (3) prevent a company from continuing to collect debts or selling the debt to others for collection; and (4) obtain an extended fraud alert.

The ID Theft Affidavit may be required by a company in order for you to obtain applications or other transaction records related to the theft of your identity. These records may help you prove that you are a victim. For example, you may be able to show that the signature on an application is not yours. These documents also may contain information about the identity thief that is valuable to law enforcement.

Instructions

This affidavit has two parts:

• Part One — the ID Theft Affidavit — is where you report general information about yourself and the theft.

• Part Two — the Fraudulent Account Statement — is where you describe the fraudulent account(s) opened in your name. Use a separate Fraudulent Account Statement for each company you need to write to.

When you send the affidavit to the companies, attach copies (NOT originals) of any supporting documents (for example, driver's license or police report). Before submitting your affidavit, review the disputed account(s) with family members or friends who may have information about the account(s) or access to them.

Complete this affidavit as soon as possible. Many creditors ask that you send it within two weeks. Delays on your part could slow the investigation.

Be as accurate and complete as possible. You may choose not to provide some of the information requested. However, incorrect or incomplete information will slow the process of investigating your claim and absolving the debt. Print clearly.

When you have finished completing the affidavit, mail a copy to each creditor, bank, or company that provided the thief with the unauthorized credit, goods, or services you describe. Attach a copy of the Fraudulent Account Statement with information only on accounts opened at the institution to which you are sending the packet, as well as any other supporting documentation you are able to provide.

Send the appropriate documents to each company by certified mail, return receipt requested, so you can prove that it was received. The companies will review your claim and send you a written response telling you the outcome of their investigation. Keep a copy of everything you submit.

If you are unable to complete the affidavit, a legal guardian or someone with power of attorney may complete it for you. Except as noted, the information you provide will be used only by the company to process your affidavit, investigate the events you report, and help stop further fraud.

If this affidavit is requested in a lawsuit, the company might have to provide it to the requesting party. Completing this affidavit does not guarantee that the identity thief will be prosecuted or that the debt will be cleared.

Sample Letters

Sample Blocking Letter to Consumer Reporting Agency

Date

Your Name
Your Address
Your City, State, Zip Code

Complaint Department
Name of Consumer Reporting Company
Address
City, State, Zip Code

Dear Sir or Madam:

I am a victim of identity theft. I am writing to request that you block the following fraudulent information in my file. This information does not relate to any transaction that I have made. The items also are circled on the attached copy of the report I received. *(Identify item(s) to be blocked by name of source, such as creditors or tax court, and identify type of item, such as credit account, judgment, etc.)*

Enclosed is a copy of the law enforcement report regarding my identity theft. Please let me know if you need any other information from me to block this information on my credit report.

Sincerely, Your name

Enclosures: *(List what you are enclosing.)*

Sample Dispute Letter for Fraudulent Charge on Credit or Debit Card

Date

Your Name
Your Address
Your City, State, Zip Code

Your Account Number

Name of Creditor
Billing Inquiries Address
City, State, Zip Code

Dear Sir or Madam:

I am writing to dispute a fraudulent (charge or debit) on my account in the amount of $xxx. I am a victim of identity theft, and I did not make this (charge or debit). I am requesting that the (charge be removed or the debit reinstated), that any finance and other charges related to the fraudulent amount be credited, as well, and that I receive an accurate statement.

Enclosed are copies of (*use this sentence to describe any enclosed information, such as a police report*) supporting my position. Please investigate this matter and correct the fraudulent (charge or debit) as soon as possible.

Sincerely, Your name

Enclosures: *(List what you are enclosing.)*

Identity Theft Affidavit

The Identity Theft Affidavit was prepared by the Federal Trade Commission (FTC) and provides a model form that can be used to report information to many companies, simplifying the process of alerting companies where a new account was opened in the victim's name. Previously, victims of identity theft often had to fill out a separate reporting form for each fraudulent account opened by the identity thief. Developed by the FTC in conjunction with banks, credit grantors and consumer advocates, the ID Theft Affidavit is accepted by participating credit issuers, retailers, banks, and other financial institutions.

Everything You Need to Know About Identity Theft

Page 1

Average time to complete: 10 minutes

Identity Theft Victim's Complaint and Affidavit

A voluntary form for filing a report with law enforcement, and disputes with credit reporting agencies and creditors about identity theft-related problems. Visit ftc.gov/idtheft to use a secure online version that you can print for your records.

Before completing this form:
1. Place a fraud alert on your credit reports, and review the reports for signs of fraud.
2. Close the accounts that you know, or believe, have been tampered with or opened fraudulently.

About You *(the victim)*

Now

(1) My full legal name: _____ First Middle Last Suffix
(2) My date of birth: _____ mm/dd/yyyy
(3) My Social Security number: ___-__-____
(4) My driver's license: _____ State Number
(5) My current street address:
_____ Number & Street Name Apartment, Suite, etc.
_____ City State Zip Code Country
(6) I have lived at this address since _____ mm/yyyy
(7) My daytime phone: (___) _____
    My evening phone: (___) _____
    My email: _____

Leave (3) blank until you provide this form to someone with a legitimate business need, like when you are filing your report at the police station or sending the form to a credit reporting agency to correct your credit report.

At the Time of the Fraud

(8) My full legal name was: _____ First Middle Last Suffix
(9) My address was: _____ Number & Street Name Apartment, Suite, etc.
_____ City State Zip Code Country
(10) My daytime phone: (___) _____ My evening phone: (___) _____
     My email: _____

Skip (8) - (10) if your information has not changed since the fraud.

The Paperwork Reduction Act requires the FTC to display a valid control number (in this case, OMB control #3084-0047) before we can collect – or sponsor the collection of – your information, or require you to provide it.

Page 2

Victim's Name _____ Phone number (___)_____ Page 2

About You *(the victim) (Continued)*

Declarations

(11) I ☐ did OR ☐ did not authorize anyone to use my name or personal information to obtain money, credit, loans, goods, or services — or for any other purpose — as described in this report.

(12) I ☐ did OR ☐ did not receive any money, goods, services, or other benefit as a result of the events described in this report.

(13) I ☐ am OR ☐ am not willing to work with law enforcement if charges are brought against the person(s) who committed the fraud.

About the Fraud

(14) I believe the following person used my information or identification documents to open new accounts, use my existing accounts, or commit other fraud.

> (14): Enter what you know about anyone you believe was involved (even if you don't have complete information).

Name: _____
          First   Middle   Last   Suffix

Address: _____
       Number & Street Name   Apartment, Suite, etc.

_____
City   State   Zip Code   Country

Phone Numbers: (___)_____ (___)_____

Additional information about this person: _____
_____
_____
_____
_____
_____
_____
_____
_____
_____

Page 3

Victim's Name _____ Phone number (___)_____ Page 3

(15) Additional information about the crime (for example, how the identity thief gained access to your information or which documents or information were used):

_____
_____
_____
_____
_____
_____
_____

> (14) and (15): Attach additional sheets as needed.

Documentation

(16) I can verify my identity with these documents:

☐ A valid government-issued photo identification card (for example, my driver's license, state-issued ID card, or my passport).
If you are under 16 and don't have a photo-ID, a copy of your birth certificate or a copy of your official school record showing your enrollment and legal address is acceptable.

☐ Proof of residency during the time the disputed charges occurred, the loan was made, or the other event took place (for example, a copy of a rental/lease agreement in my name, a utility bill, or an insurance bill).

> (16): Reminder: Attach copies of your identity documents when sending this form to creditors and credit reporting agencies.

About the Information or Accounts

(17) The following personal information (like my name, address, Social Security number, or date of birth) in my credit report is inaccurate as a result of this identity theft:

(A) _____
(B) _____
(C) _____

(18) Credit inquiries from these companies appear on my credit report as a result of this identity theft:

Company Name: _____
Company Name: _____
Company Name: _____

Page 4

Victim's Name _____ Phone number (___) _____ Page 4

(19) Below are details about the different frauds committed using my personal information.

Name of Institution	Contact Person	Phone	Extension

Account Number _____ Routing Number _____ Affected Check Number(s) _____

Account Type: ☐ Credit ☐ Bank ☐ Phone/Utilities ☐ Loan
☐ Government Benefits ☐ Internet or Email ☐ Other

Select ONE:
☐ This account was opened fraudulently.
☐ This was an existing account that someone tampered with.

Date Opened or Misused (mm/yyyy) _____ Date Discovered (mm/yyyy) _____ Total Amount Obtained ($) _____

Name of Institution	Contact Person	Phone	Extension

Account Number _____ Routing Number _____ Affected Check Number(s) _____

Account Type: ☐ Credit ☐ Bank ☐ Phone/Utilities ☐ Loan
☐ Government Benefits ☐ Internet or Email ☐ Other

Select ONE:
☐ This account was opened fraudulently.
☐ This was an existing account that someone tampered with.

Date Opened or Misused (mm/yyyy) _____ Date Discovered (mm/yyyy) _____ Total Amount Obtained ($) _____

Name of Institution	Contact Person	Phone	Extension

Account Number _____ Routing Number _____ Affected Check Number(s) _____

Account Type: ☐ Credit ☐ Bank ☐ Phone/Utilities ☐ Loan
☐ Government Benefits ☐ Internet or Email ☐ Other

Select ONE:
☐ This account was opened fraudulently.
☐ This was an existing account that someone tampered with.

Date Opened or Misused (mm/yyyy) _____ Date Discovered (mm/yyyy) _____ Total Amount Obtained ($) _____

(19): If there were more than three frauds, copy this page blank, and attach as many additional copies as necessary.

Enter any applicable information that you have, even if it is incomplete or an estimate.

If the thief committed two types of fraud at one company, list the company twice, giving the information about the two frauds separately.

Contact Person: Someone you dealt with, whom an investigator can call about this fraud.

Account Number: The number of the credit or debit card, bank account, loan, or other account that was misused.

Dates: Indicate when the thief began to misuse your information and when you discovered the problem.

Amount Obtained: For instance, the total amount purchased with the card or withdrawn from the account.

Page 5

Victim's Name _____ Phone number (___)_____ Page 5

Your Law Enforcement Report

(20) One way to get a credit reporting agency to quickly block identity theft-related information from appearing on your credit report is to submit a detailed law enforcement report ("Identity Theft Report"). You can obtain an Identity Theft Report by taking this form to your local law enforcement office, along with your supporting documentation. Ask an officer to witness your signature and complete the rest of the information in this section. It's important to get your report number, whether or not you are able to file in person or get a copy of the official law enforcement report. Attach a copy of any confirmation letter or official law enforcement report you receive when sending this form to credit reporting agencies.

Select ONE:
- ☐ I have not filed a law enforcement report.
- ☐ I was unable to file any law enforcement report.
- ☐ I filed an automated report with the law enforcement agency listed below.
- ☐ I filed my report in person with the law enforcement officer and agency listed below.

(20): Check "I have not..." If you have not yet filed a report with law enforcement or you have chosen not to. Check "I was unable..." if you tried to file a report but law enforcement refused to take it.

Automated report: A law enforcement report filed through an automated system, for example, by telephone, mail, or the Internet, instead of a face-to-face interview with a law enforcement officer.

_____   _____
Law Enforcement Department   State

_____   _____
Report Number   Filing Date (mm/dd/yyyy)

_____   _____
Officer's Name (please print)   Officer's Signature

_____   (___)_____
Badge Number   Phone Number

Did the victim receive a copy of the report from the law enforcement officer?   ☐ Yes   OR   ☐ No

Victim's FTC complaint number (if available): _____

Page 6

Victim's Name _____ Phone number (___) _____ Page 6

Signature

As applicable, sign and date *IN THE PRESENCE OF* a law enforcement officer, a notary, or a witness.

(21) I certify that, to the best of my knowledge and belief, all of the information on and attached to this complaint is true, correct, and complete and made in good faith. I understand that this complaint or the information it contains may be made available to federal, state, and/or local law enforcement agencies for such action within their jurisdiction as they deem appropriate. I understand that knowingly making any false or fraudulent statement or representation to the government may violate federal, state, or local criminal statutes, and may result in a fine, imprisonment, or both.

_____ _____
Signature   Date Signed (mm/dd/yyyy)

Your Affidavit

(22) If you do not choose to file a report with law enforcement, you may use this form as an Identity Theft Affidavit to prove to each of the companies where the thief misused your information that you are not responsible for the fraud. While many companies accept this affidavit, others require that you submit different forms. Check with each company to see if it accepts this form. You should also check to see if it requires notarization. If so, sign in the presence of a notary. If it does not, please have one witness (non-relative) sign that you completed and signed this Affidavit.

_____
Notary

Witness:

_____ _____
Signature   Printed Name

_____ _____
Date   Telephone Number

83